The Little Gardeners Guide

Niki Horin

Alicat

Contents

Grow it and gobble it! 38

Make-and-do gardening fun! 50

How to be a little gardener

Being a little gardener is all about growing and caring for plants. With a little bit of work and a lot of dirty fun, you can create your very own garden. Best of all, you don't even need to have a garden! You can grow plants in pots and other containers. Before you get started, it is important to collect your equipment.

Little gardener clothes

A hat – to protect your face from the sun

SUNCREEN LOTION

Plenty of sunscreen lotion – to protect your skin from the sun

Sunglasses – to protect your eyes from the sun

Gloves – to protect your hands from dirt, scrapes and cuts

Gumboots – to protect your feet from water and dirt

Little gardener tools

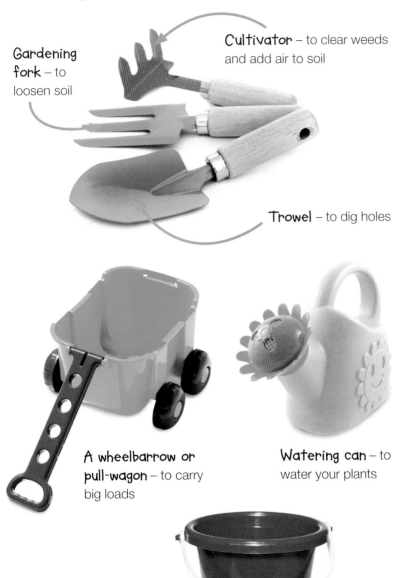

Gardening fork – to loosen soil

Cultivator – to clear weeds and add air to soil

Trowel – to dig holes

A wheelbarrow or pull-wagon – to carry big loads

Watering can – to water your plants

Bucket – to move around soil, rocks and other small things

Be safe!

There are a couple of tips you should always remember when gardening:

- Adult-size tools are too big for your hands and might be dangerous – only use child-size gardening tools
- Only use gardening tools when an adult is present
- Always be careful when using your gardening tools
- Do not leave your tools lying around
- Do not leave your tools in the rain where they might get damaged

Once you've read this chapter, jump into your gumboots and explore the amazing world just past your doorstep!

Be a garden explorer!

Look out the window. Does it seem pretty quiet out there? Look closer. Your garden is alive with activity! Flowers are blooming, plants are growing, and animals are busily going about their day above and below the soil. Your garden is an exciting world waiting for you to discover its secrets! But what do you know about your garden and how it works?

The information on the following pages will help you answer some of the big questions about what goes on in the garden.

What's in the garden?

Gardens are full of amazing things! Some are living, like plants and animals, and some are non-living, like soil and water. All of these things are important parts of a garden.

Water

Water is a non-living thing. Most of the water in gardens comes straight from the sky – as rain!

Many people don't have gardens. Instead, they grow plants in pots filled with soil. Lots of different plants can be grown in pots.

Splashing in rain puddles is fun to do!

Plants

Plants are living things that grow. Different plants come in different sizes. Some plants, like trees, grow very tall. Other plants, like grasses, are often small.

For more information about the different types of plants, see pages 12 and 13.

Mother bird

Baby birds calling for their lunch

Bird nests are built high up in trees

Bird nests are made from sticks, leaves, twigs, hair and bird spit!

Animals and their homes

Animals are living things. There are many animals that make their homes in gardens. Worms live under the soil. Spiders and lizards often live under rocks or under the bark of a tree. Birds and bees build their own homes in trees. Beetles and bugs live on plant leaves.

Soil

Soil is a non-living thing. It is made up of very old rocks and very old plants. Over thousands of years, rocks and the remains of plants break up into tiny pieces to become soil.

What are plants?

Plants are living things, just like you and me. But they don't have legs, so they can't move. Instead, plants live in the soil. They have roots under the ground that hold onto the soil. Above ground, we can see the stem and leaves of plants.

All plants have:
• a stem
• leaves
• roots

What the stem, leaves and roots look like depends on what type of plant you are looking at.

Some plants have flowers

Stem

Leaves

Roots

Why are plants important?

Plants are important for all living things on Earth. Plants provide homes and food, and also help keep the air fresh.

Plants as animal homes

Plants provide homes to animals of all sizes – from large to teeny tiny! Orangutans, birds, snakes and ladybug beetles are just some of the animals that like to live on plants!

Plants as food

Plants provide food for many of Earth's animals, including us! Cows like to eat plants, especially grass. Humans like to eat lots of fruit and vegetables. All the fruit and vegetables we eat come from plants.

For more information about how plants clean the air, see page 16.

Plants clean the air

Plants absorb the carbon dioxide in the air and release it as oxygen. Animals and humans need oxygen to breathe.

Different types of plants

Planet Earth is full of plants! There are many thousands of different plants, so they are put into groups to help people more easily identify them. Each plant group contains plants that share features, or look similar. Knowing some of these groups will help you work out what type of plant you are looking at!

Trees

Trees are the world's largest plants! The stem of a tree is called a trunk and is made of wood.

Grasses

Grasses are plants with long thin leaves. Grass is often seen in gardens growing together. Lots of grass makes lawn.

All these fruit and vegetables come from plants.

Fruit and vegetables

All fruit and vegetables come from plants. Fruit and vegetables are the parts of a plant that we eat.

Flowers

Some plants grow flowers. The flowering part of plants is made up of beautiful petals.

Succulents

Some plants store water. These are called succulents (*say* suk-u-lents). Cactus plants are popular succulents. The leaves of a cactus are called branches and are covered in spines.

Ferns

Ferns are plants with pretty leaves called fronds. Fern fronds can be very large or very small.

13

Where do plants come from?

You don't need to buy seeds from the shop to grow plants. You can collect seeds from your food or use parts of other plants to grow new ones!

New plants come from other plants. Most plants grow from the seeds or spores that grow inside other plants. Some plants start life as 'cuttings', or parts, of other plants.

Plants from seeds

Many grasses, trees and flowering plants grow from seeds. Seeds can come in all different shapes and sizes.

Pumpkin seeds

Avocado seed

Tomato seeds

Plants from spores

Some mosses, ferns and funguses grow from spores.

Millions of spores grow in spore cases under a fern's fronds, or leaves.

Plants from cuttings

Not all new plants grow from seeds or spores. Sometimes, new plants can grow from cuttings of other plants. A new cactus can grow from a 'branch' of another cactus plant. A new onion can grow from an onion bulb. A new strawberry plant can grow from a strawberry plant runner.

A new cactus can grow from a branch cut from another cactus.

From flower to fruit

Fruit comes from flowers. The 'fruit' of a plant can only develop after a flower has been pollinated. Pollination is the transfer of pollen from one plant to another plant of the same species. Once the flower has been pollinated, it dies and a fruit grows in its place. Seeds grow inside the fruit.

An apple tree grows flowers. These flowers are pollinated.

After pollination, the flower dies and the fruit begins to grow.

The seeds of an apple tree are stored inside the fruit. We call apple seeds 'pips'.

The pollinators

Some flowering plants self-pollinate, while others need help from animals to carry their pollen from one plant to another. A number of animals help pollinate plants, but the greatest pollinators are bees! As they visit flowers to collect nectar for their honey making, pollen sticks to the bee's hairy legs. The bee then takes this pollen to the next flower it visits. The wind is also a pollinator, carrying seeds and spores to new places.

As bees visit flowers, they also pollinate them!

How do plants eat?

All living things need food to grow, but plants don't have mouths, so they can't eat like you and me. Instead, plants make their own food inside their special plant parts. Plants need water, soil, air and sunlight to make food. The way plants make food is called photosynthesis (*say* fotto-sin-thee-sus).

The plant food recipe

Photosynthesis is really just a big word for the recipe plants use to make food. The main ingredients are water, soil and air. The sun provides the energy needed to mix these ingredients.

Water

Water is important to all living things. The water used in plant food falls from the sky as rain or from your watering can. This water soaks into the soil.

Soil

Soil is full of nutrients that help keep plants healthy. It also contains water that has soaked into the soil. The plant uses its roots to drink nutrients and water from the soil.

Air

The sky is filled with air. Air is full of a gas called carbon dioxide. The plant's leaves breathe in carbon dioxide. Plants use part of this gas, the carbon, to make food. Plants breathe out the rest of the gas as oxygen.

Sunlight

To mix the ingredients of a cake you need electric energy to power your blender. To mix the ingredients from soil, water and air into plant food, plants use energy from the sun.

Through photosynthesis, a plant mixes carbon from the air with water and nutrients from the soil to make food. The sun gives a plant the energy it needs to make food.

The sun's energy comes to Earth as heat and light.

Water soaks into the soil.

The plant breathes in carbon dioxide through its leaves.

Tiny cells in the plant's leaves absorb sunlight and use the sun's energy to mix the ingredients of plant food.

The plant uses its roots to drink water and nutrients from the soil.

How do seedlings grow from seeds?

A baby plant is called a seedling. The growth of a seed into a seedling can take as little as a week. This growth requires good airy soil, enough water, and heat from the sun. The growth of a plant from seed to seedling is called 'germination'.

From seed to seedling in four steps!

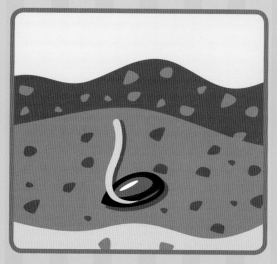

1. The seed is planted or covered in good airy soil. At this stage, the seed contains all the food that it needs to grow. Seeds cannot make their own food because they don't have leaves.

2. If there is enough water, air and warmth in the soil, a plant shoot will soon grow from the seed. This shoot will grow towards the warmth of the sun.

What would happen if plants received no water or sunlight?

Plants need air, soil, water and sunlight to grow. If they don't have these things, they die.

These first leaves are called 'seed' leaves. They look quite different from the 'true' leaves of a plant.

3 As the seed pushes through the soil, its seed coat will fall off and its first leaves will appear. Now that leaves have formed, the plant can start to make its own food, through photosynthesis. With food, it grows quickly – the stem grows and so do the roots.

4 Soon after the 'seed' leaves have grown, the first 'true' leaves of the plant will appear. These are the leaves that adult plants have. With the right conditions, this little seedling will eventually grow flowers and fruit!

19

What animals are in the garden?

Many types of animals live in gardens. All animals have their own special role to play in nature, but sometimes animals can be annoying in gardens, especially when they feed on plants' roots, fruit, leaves and juices. To take care of your plants, it's important to know which animals are good for your garden and which animals are downright naughty!

The good ones!

Bees

Bees are important pollinators and are very good for your garden. They also make delicious honey! But bees aren't good for you if you get stung – so keep your distance!

Worms

All gardeners love worms! Worms eat soil and when it comes out the other end the quality of the soil is improved, which is great for your plants. Worms are so good for gardens that gardeners sometimes build worm farms. These farms provide nutrient-rich soil.

To find out how to build your own worm farm, see pages 58 and 59.

Frogs

If you are lucky enough to have a pond in your garden, you might also have frogs. Frogs help in the garden by eating lots of plant-feeding insects before the insects can feed on your plants!

Dragonflies

Dragonflies are insects that have been around since the days of the dinosaurs! These amazing hunters catch plant-feeding insects while flying through the air.

21

Butterflies

Butterflies are very well behaved garden visitors and help to pollinate flowers. It is always a treat to see a beautiful butterfly in the garden.

Birds

Most birds do a good job eating plant-feeding insects in the garden, especially snails and slugs. But many birds gobble fruit and seedlings too. A scarecrow can help keep birds away from fruit and seedlings.

Praying mantids

Praying mantids are the coolest-looking insects around! These camouflaged hunters do great work in the garden eating all kinds of plant-feeding insects, including aphids and beetles.

To find out how to make your own scarecrow, see page 57.

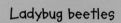 Ladybug beetles

Ladybug beetles are very good to have in the garden. They eat aphids and other plant-feeding insects. There are lots of different types of ladybugs. The only naughty one is the 28-spotted ladybug that likes to munch on leaves – so always count the spots!

Spiders

Spiders play an important role in the garden by gobbling plant-feeding insects. Not all spiders live in webs, some live under rocks or among the leaf litter. Always keep your distance from spiders because some will bite if they get frightened.

Centipedes

Centipedes hunt lots of insects including naughty plant-feeding slugs and snails. But centipedes can bite, so leave them alone and let them do their important job in the garden.

The naughty ones!

Naughty animals in the garden eat leaves and fruit, suck juices from plants and chew on the roots. A small number of naughty animals usually isn't a problem, but it is important to know which ones these animals are and how to deal with them in case their numbers increase.

Aphids

Aphids are tiny insects that suck the juices out of plants, especially roses and citrus trees. Ladybug beetles can eat lots of aphids in one meal. If there aren't any ladybug beetles around, you can wash the aphids from your plants with water.

Snails and slugs

Snails and slugs eat new leaves on plants. They are sneaky gobblers that come out at night. One way to protect your new plants from snails and slugs is to sprinkle sawdust or eggshells around your seedlings.

Fruit flies

Fruit flies damage fruit. The female fruit fly lays her eggs by 'stinging' them into apples, pears and other fruit. When her babies are born they grow inside the fruit and feed on it, causing it to rot on the tree. The best way to protect your plants from fruit flies is to cover the fruit with a paper bag.

Caterpillars

Caterpillars eat the leaves and roots of plants. Caterpillars are the chubby babies of moths and butterflies. These bright wrigglers have little in common with their winged parents. One major difference is that caterpillars have jaws and can gobble away leaves and roots in no time. The best way to get rid of caterpillars is to pick them off your plants. But always use gloves, as the hairs on their bodies can cause a nasty sting.

Stink bugs

Stink bugs suck the juice from citrus fruit, like oranges and lemons. There are lots of different types of stink bug and most are quite large. The best way to stop them sucking on fruit is to move them. But always use gloves and wear sunglasses. Stink bugs spray a stinky liquid when they are frightened, which will sting if it gets in your eyes.

Once you've read this chapter, you're ready to use your little gardener skills!

Get into gardening!

Plants are like pets. Of course, you must make sure they have enough soil, air and light to make their food. But like pets, plants don't only need food to be healthy and happy – they need YOU! You need to protect, water, weed, mulch, thin and support your plants as they grow. Gardening sure is a lot of work, but the fun of creating your very own garden will be worth your toil in the soil!

The information on the following pages explains gardening basics and how to care for your plants.

Planning your garden

Plants can grow almost anywhere! You just need to decide where to start your garden – in pots or in a garden plot? If you don't have a garden the answer is simple – in pots! If you do have a garden, it is usually best to sow all your seeds in pots first and then move seedlings into the plot later on.

Preparing your garden plot

You will need to do some work to prepare the garden plot for your plants.

To find out how to make your own compost, see pages 58, 59 and 60.

Clearing the plot

You will need to clear the area of weeds and aerate (add air) to the soil. Use your garden fork to loosen the soil and your cultivator to clear weeds and aerate the soil.

Preparing the soil for your plants

You will need to work out whether the soil in your garden plot is sandy soil or clay soil. Have a close look. Sandy soil has lots of coarse pieces. Clay soil has lots of fine particles. It's better to have sandy soil as this helps the water drain through the soil properly. You may need to add compost to your garden plot to help improve the quality of the soil for your new plants.

28

A garden plot has lots of room to grow!

Preparing your pots

If you want to grow your plants in pots, the first thing to do is collect the pots. You will need lots of them because plants need to be re-potted into larger pots as they grow.

Collecting pots

You will need many pots in lots of different sizes. But don't worry, there's no need to buy new pots from the store. First, ask your family and friends if they have any spare pots or hanging baskets you can use. Then, search around the recycling bin and around the house for different containers that can be used. You can use small tubs for growing seedlings, ice-cream tubs, plastic bottles or even an old shoe or old toy truck for larger plants. Buckets and even washing baskets can be used for really big plants! Try to find the most interesting and unusual containers for a really amazing garden!

Preparing the pots for your plants

Once you've collected all your pots and containers, there are some steps you need to follow to get them ready for your plants.

1. Clean all your pots and containers.

2. Once your pots are clean, it's time to decorate them!

For ideas on how to decorate your pots and containers, see page 52.

3. When you have finished decorating your pots and containers, **ask an adult** to help punch some holes in the bottom of the pots. These holes are important because they drain out the extra water that your plant doesn't need.

4. Cover the holes in the bottom of your pots with stones, so the water won't drain straight out the bottom when you water your plants.

5. Fill your small pots with rich compost and/or potting mix.

29

A tiny seedling sprouting from the soil

Growing plants from seeds

If you are growing plants from seeds, it is often best to sow your seeds in small pots that are kept inside to protect them from bad weather and hungry snails, slugs and caterpillars. When seeds grow into seedlings, you can move them into larger pots or your garden plot.

For advice on growing strong, healthy plants, see pages 40 and 41.

1 Fill a small pot or container (with holes in the base) with potting mix or compost. Push a small hole about half a finger deep into the soil.

2 Add two seeds into the hole and gently push some surrounding soil over the hole. Water gently. Place the pot on a windowsill.

3 When the seeds germinate, remove the weaker of the two seedlings. This will allow enough room for the strongest seedling to grow.

4 To move your plant to a bigger home, carefully tip the plant out with its soil – don't damage the plant. Once your plant is re-potted, pat the soil around it and water it in gently.

5 The amount you water your plant will depend on what type of plant it is.

6 Follow the instructions on the seed packet about how to care for your growing plant.

Protecting your plants

To keep your plants healthy and strong, you will need to protect them from hungry plant-feeding animals and bad weather. The best way to protect your plants depends on where they are growing.

In pots

It's easy to protect pot plants from animals and bad weather. You can move your pots high up – far away from the reach of hungry animals, and/or you can move your pots inside away from frost, wind, rain or storms.

Without your protection, caterpillars, slugs and snails can quickly gobble plants!

In a garden plot

Plant-feeding animals and bad weather can damage plants in garden plots. Plants in garden plots can't be moved, so you might need to build some protection for them.

The easiest way to build protection is to create a barrier around each of your plants:

1. Find a clear plastic drink bottle that is larger than your plant.

2. **Ask an adult** to cut off the top of the bottle and then to make a hole at the base of the bottle.

3. Place the bottle over the top of your plant. Be careful not to squash the stem or leaves.

4. When the bottle is over your plant, push the bottle firmly into the soil.

Now your plant is snug as a bug in a rug and super safe! Repeat these steps for every plant in your plot. Importantly, your plants will still receive sunlight through the clear plastic and air through the hole in the top of the bottle!

For more about plant-feeding animals, see pages 24 and 25.

To protect new fruit on your plant from birds and other animals, cover the fruit with netting, like the material from an orange bag, or you could use a paper bag.

33

Watering your plants

It's best to water your plants in the morning, but not every day. Instead, water your plants with a lot of water every few days. To water your plants you should carefully aim your watering can at the soil, not the plant! Watering straight onto the plant can damage new growth.

Always use a watering can, as this will help you control the amount of water you give your plants.

Weeding your plants

Weeds are nuisance plants. They are plants you didn't plant – and you really don't want them! Weeds grow fast and can quickly take all the water, light and nutrients your plants need to grow. You must remove weeds or else they will kill your plants. Always pull weeds out at the root. You may need your trowel to remove stubborn weeds. Creating plant labels with the names of your plants will help you identify weeds from plants!

To make your own plant labels, see pages 54 and 55.

Mulching your plants

Mulch is a protective layer that sits on top of the soil around your plants. It is usually compost or straw. Mulch helps to keep your plants warm and stops weeds from taking root in the soil. It also helps to stop the soil from drying out. You should add mulch to the soil after it has been weeded and watered.

Thinning your plants

Thinning is something you do to make room for plants to grow. As they grow bigger, your plants will need more room. If your seedlings or plants look like they are going to get crowded, you will need to move some of them to another pot or a different part of your plot. If you have too many plants you might need to throw some away. Only throw away the smallest, weakest plants. Throw unwanted plants into your compost bin if you have one.

Thinning your plants is important because it gives them room to grow!

Supporting your plants

Some plants need help standing up, especially those that grow tall or grow lots of heavy fruit. Plants like tomatoes and climbing roses often need help standing up. You can support your plants with stakes or trellises.

Stake

To support your plants, you may need a stake, like a bamboo pole or a sturdy stick.

To use a stake:

1. **Ask an adult** to stick the stake into the soil next to your plant. Be careful not to disturb the roots or damage your plant. It is best to stick the stake in the soil when the plant is young and the roots are small.

2. Using string, tie the stem of the plant (not too tightly) to the stake.

3. As your plant grows, support new growth by tying it to the stake.

TOMATO
Grosse Lisse

Always **ask an adult** to help with stakes and trellises, and be sure to protect your eyes from the ends of the stake or trellis.

Trellis

A trellis is another way to support plants. It is often used to support climbing roses or vines. A trellis is often attached to a fence, but can also be stuck in the soil of a pot or garden plot.

To use a trellis:

1. **Ask an adult** to attach the trellis to a fence or to push it deeply in the soil.

2. To attach your plant to the trellis, wind the stem among the cross-hatching of the trellis.

3. As your plant grows, 'train' it up the trellis by winding new growth among the cross-hatching.

Use the instructions in this chapter as a basic guide to growing your own plants. You may need to adjust them to suit the particular conditions of your garden and where you live.

Grow it and gobble it!

Now that you know about what goes on in the garden and how to care for plants, you're ready to grow your own plants! And the best plants to grow are the ones you can gobble!

The information on the following pages will help you to grow fresh fruit and vegetables at home.

Grow strong, healthy plants

It's a fact of gardening that seeds, seedlings or plants sometimes don't grow. Growing strong, healthy plants requires the right conditions and the right care. Every plant needs different conditions and care. Working out what works and what doesn't is part of the fun of gardening!

Why plants sometimes don't grow

Plants may not grow because:

- seeds aren't suited to grow in the area where you live
- seeds or seedlings are sowed at the wrong time of year
- seeds or seedlings are damaged by weather or animals
- soil is not right for the plant
- plants are under-watered or overwatered
- plants receive too much or not enough sunlight

For more information about
- how to care for your plants, see pages 32 to 37
- which animals you need to protect your plants from, see pages 24 and 25
- how to prepare pots for plants, see page 29
- how to grow plants from seeds, see pages 30 and 31.

Plant-growing tips

The right conditions and care

Seed packets and seedling labels are full of useful information about the special set of conditions and care a plant needs to grow healthy and strong. If you're not sure that your garden has the right conditions for a particular plant variety, ask the nursery staff.

The right type of soil

Fruit and vegetable plants grow best in light, crumbly soil with lots of air and nutrients in it. If the soil conditions are not right in your garden, you can add liquid plant food or compost, or you can grow your plants in pots and use special soil called potting mix.

Shelter your plants

Plants should be grown in a sheltered spot, so they can't be damaged by wind, storms, frost and other weather or be overwatered by rain.

Don't forget to water your plants!

The right amount of sunlight

All plants need sunlight, but some plants are more sensitive to sunlight than others. How much sunlight your plant needs depends on what variety of plant it is. Again, read the seed packet or label to find out this information.

Grow alfalfa

Alfalfa sprouts are fast and easy to grow. They don't need sunlight, soil or pots!

You will need:

- A handful of alfalfa seeds
- A glass jar with a heavy base and wide neck
- A piece of muslin
- An elastic band
- Water

When to plant:

Any time of year

Sunlight:

No sun required. Grow in warm dark place, like a cupboard

Watering:

Twice a day, see steps 3 and 5

Protect them from:

No protection needed

How long until you see an alfalfa sprout?

Within a week

What to do:

1. Put all the seeds into the glass jar.

2. Using the muslin, cover the mouth of the jar. While you hold the muslin in place, **ask an adult** to put an elastic band across the neck of the jar to hold the muslin in place.

3. Pour water through the muslin, until the jar is half full. Now, carefully turn the jar upside-down, holding the muslin in place and pour out the water.

4. Put the jar in a warm, dark place.

5. Twice a day wet the seeds as explained in step 3.

6. When your alfalfa sprouts have grown, wash well before eating them.

How to gobble alfalfa!

Alfalfa is a tasty, healthy snack on its own, or you can add it to salads or a sandwich for some extra crunch!

Alfalfa sprouts are one of the easiest foods to grow.

Grow strawberries

You can grow strawberry plants easily from cuttings called 'runners'. Be warned, your strawberry plants will grow in all directions! But instead of trying to control your plants by staking them, why not grow strawberries in hanging baskets and let them grow wild?

What to do:

1 Use the cardboard to line the inside of the hanging basket.

2 Add soil to the hanging basket.

3 Use the watering can to completely soak the soil.

4 Make a number of small holes in the soil and plant the roots of each strawberry runner. Cover with soil and water in well.

5 Hang the basket in a sunny, sheltered spot.

6 Weed your hanging basket often.

How to gobble strawberries!

Strawberries are delicious straight from the plant, or sliced on top of pancakes!

You will need:
- A hanging basket
- Potting mix
- Cardboard
- 6 strawberry runners
- Water

When to plant:
Winter

Sunlight:
Full sun – at least 6 hours of sunlight a day

Watering:
Water once or twice a week

Protect them from:
Birds, snails and slugs

How long until you see a strawberry?
About 2 months

Strawberries aren't ready to eat until they are red. The redder the strawberry is, the sweeter it will be!

43

Grow carrots

Carrots are tasty raw or cooked. Carrots are the swollen roots of the plant that grow under the ground. You will know your plants are growing when you see their stalks coming out of the soil!

What to do:

1. Use your pencil to press a line into the soil about half a finger deep.

2. Sprinkle the seeds along the line and cover with a thin layer of soil.

3. Press down soil and water in gently.

4. Keep well watered for 7 to 10 days, until seedlings appear.

5. If the seedlings are crowded, pull the weak ones out so the stronger ones have room to grow. The plants should be one hand's length apart.

6. When the stalks reach two hand lengths tall, pull one out to check if the carrots are forming – keep checking until they are ready!

How to gobble carrots!

Carrots are delicious straight from the soil (don't forget to wash the dirt off!) or you can add them to salads, or make delicious carrot soup!

Baby carrots are sweeter than full-grown carrots.

Grow cherry tomatoes

Cherry tomatoes are delicious tiny tomatoes. These plants grow in all directions! It's best to use a stake to support tomato plants.

What to do:

1. Dig a hole in the soil.

2. Carefully tip out the seedling and place it in the hole.

3. Press the soil down around the roots and water in well.

4. **Ask an adult** to push the stake into the soil, but avoid pushing it near the plant's roots. As your plant grows, gently tie the stem to the stake.

5. Mulch with straw or compost.

6. Keep your plant in a sunny spot.

7. You'll know it's time to harvest when you see your plant covered in plump red tomatoes!

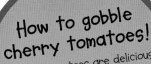

How to gobble cherry tomatoes!

Cherry tomatoes are delicious straight from the vine, but you can also add them to your salads, pizzas or pasta sauce!

You will need:
- A medium-size pot
- Potting mix
- A tomato seedling
- A stake
- String
- Water

When to plant:
Mid-spring to mid-summer

Sunlight:
Full sun – at least 6 hours of sunlight a day

Watering:
2 to 3 times a week

Protect them from:
Caterpillars and aphids

How long until you see a tomato?
About 3 months

Tomatoes aren't ripe until they're red!

Grow potatoes

Potatoes are tasty vegetables that can be prepared in many different ways. This vegetable grows underground. The part of the plant we eat is at the end of the root. One potato can grow lots of them!

You will need:

- A potato that is beginning to sprout
- A bucket or a bin, with holes at the bottom for drainage
- Potting mix
- Water

When to plant:

At any warm time of the year

Sunlight:

Full sun – at least 6 hours of sunlight a day

Watering:

Water often to keep soil moist

Protect them from:

Beetles

How long until you see a potato?

About 4 months

What to do:

1 Fill container one-third full with soil.

2 Put the potato on top and then cover with soil.

3 Water in well.

4 As the plant's stem and leaves grow, add more potting mix, so the stem is always covered.

5 After the plant flowers, 'fruit' may appear. Don't eat these – they are poisonous.

6 Soon after flowering the plant will start to die – this is the time to tip over the container and count your potatoes!

How to gobble potatoes!

Boiled potatoes make mushy mash, fried potatoes make crispy chips, and baked potatoes are fun to fill!

Never eat potatoes raw and never eat green potatoes (they are poisonous).

Grow lettuce

There's nothing like fresh, crisp lettuce to add some healthy crunch to your meals. Lettuce can be grown in pots, but it is important to give each plant plenty of room to grow.

What to do:

1 Use a pencil to press a line into the soil.

2 Sprinkle seeds along the line and cover with a thin layer of soil.

3 Press down the soil and water in well.

4 When the seedlings appear, carefully move each plant to its own pot and water in well.

5 Add hard mulch, like gravel or shells to protect the layer of soil around each plant.

6 When the leaves are large and crisp, they are ready to eat. Pick them off leaf by leaf as you need them. The plant will grow more leaves.

7 When the plant grows a big thick stalk in the centre, it's time to throw the plant on the compost and grow new lettuce.

How to gobble lettuce!

Lettuce must be washed well. Once washed, it's ready to go in your sandwich or salad!

You will need:

- A medium-size pot to grow seedlings
- Potting mix
- Pencil
- Lettuce seeds
- Water

When to plant:
Spring and summer

Sunlight:
Shaded spot ok, but full sun for at least some of the day

Watering:
Water daily to keep soil moist

Protect them from:
Snails, slugs and caterpillars

How long until you see lettuce?
About 2 to 3 months

Lettuce comes in lots of different varieties.

Grow beans

There are so many different types of beans – French beans, kidney beans and broad beans just to name a few. Growing your very own curvy, bendy, monster-size beanstalk is lots of fun … just don't try to climb it!

You will need:
- 4 bean seeds
- A huge pot
- 4 stakes
- Potting mix
- String
- Water

When to plant:
Early spring

Sunlight:
Shaded spot ok, but full sun for at least some of the day

Watering:
Water daily to keep soil moist

Protect them from:
Slugs

How long until you see a bean?
Around 3 to 5 months

What to do:

1. **Ask an adult** to push the four stakes (about three hands' length apart) into the soil and tie them together at the top with string, like a wigwam.

2. Sow a bean seed next to each stake, by pushing the seed a finger deep into the soil.

3. Cover seeds with soil and water in well.

4. As the plants grow, wind the stem of each plant around its stake.

5. Once the plants have flowered, beans will soon grow. Pick the beans when they are still young and crisp. The more beans you pick, the more they will grow!

How to gobble beans!
There are many different varieties of beans, and many are delicious in soups!

Beans come in lots of different shapes and sizes!

Grow lemons

Lemons grow on trees. It can take around 8 years to grow a lemon tree from seed – so let's start with a baby lemon tree.

What to do:

1 Fill your pot with citrus potting mix.

2 Make a hole in the soil that is at least twice as deep as the plant's roots.

3 **Ask an adult** to help you carefully move the plant from its original pot to your new pot.

4 Carefully fill the area around the plant with soil.

5 Now, water the plant in well. This is very important because it helps to pack the soil tightly against the roots of the tree.

6 Add a layer of soft mulch on top of the soil.

7 Flowers will appear around springtime. Once pollinated, the plant will soon grow fruit.

How to gobble lemons!

Lemons are a sour fruit that are used to add zing to many dishes. Lemons can easily be sweetened up with some sugar and water to make delicious homemade lemonade!

Lemons are ready to be picked when they are completely yellow.

You will need:
- A young lemon tree plant
- Citrus potting mix
- Huge pot
- Water
- Soft mulch

When to plant:
Any time of year, but avoid moving plants when they are flowering or fruiting

Sunlight:
Full sun – at least 6 hours of sunlight a day

Watering:
After watered in, not often. Only water when the topsoil is dry

Protect them from:
Fruit flies and other insects

How long until you see a lemon?
Most likely in spring

Once you've read this chapter, get busy making and doing!

Sophie's spring onions!

Make-and-do gardening fun!

Being a little gardener is not just about growing plants. It's also about making the garden your very own! There are lots of fun and easy things you can do to make your garden a special place for you and your plants!

The fun make-and-do suggestions on the following pages will keep you busy for hours, even when you're not in the garden!

Paint your own pots

Painting your own pots and containers is a great way to brighten up your garden. You can paint lots of crazy patterns or paint cool pictures!

You will need:

- Somewhere to paint (**ask an adult** where you can paint)
- Painting smock, or old clothes
- Your pots and containers
- Children's paints (non-toxic, waterproof)
- Paintbrushes of different sizes
- Jar with water to rinse your paintbrushes
- Old newspaper

What to do:

1 Once you've set up your painting station, carefully paint a pattern or picture onto a pot.

2 When you have finished painting, let your painted pot dry.

3 It is important to keep your wet pot somewhere high up away from animals and where no-one will touch it.

4 When the pot is dry, it is ready to become a bright new home for one of your plants!

Write WET PAINT on the newspaper underneath your wet pot, so nobody will touch it until it is dry.

Make your own decorative mulch

Mulch provides a protective layer for your soil. You should use compost or straw as soft mulch, but hard mulch can be anything you like! Do you collect shells when you visit the beach? If so, you can use these as hard mulch. Painting shells is fun and easy to do.

What to do:

1 Once you've set up your painting station, carefully paint a pattern or picture onto each of your shells.

2 When you have finished painting, let your painted shells dry.

3 It is important to keep your wet shells somewhere high up away from animals and where no-one will touch them.

4 When your shells are dry, lay them over the soil in your pots or plot!

You will need:
- Somewhere to paint (**ask an adult** where you can paint)
- Painting smock, or old clothes
- Lots of shells
- Children's paints (non-toxic, waterproof)
- Paintbrushes of different sizes
- Jar with water to rinse your paintbrushes
- Old newspaper

For more about mulch, see page 35.

Make your own plant labels

Plant labels are very helpful to remind you which plant is which. Plant labels can be as basic as a lollipop stick with the plant name written on it, or you can make your very own cool and unusual plant labels!

You will need:

- Somewhere to paint (**ask an adult** where you can paint)
- Painting smock, or old clothes
- A plastic bottle
- Wooden skewers
- Serrated cardboard (like the lid of a pizza box)
- Children's glue (non-toxic)
- Children's paints (non-toxic, waterproof)
- Paintbrushes of different sizes
- Jar with water to rinse your paintbrushes
- Old newspaper

Plant labels are handy to help you identify your plants from weeds!

If your plant label is going to be outside, make it waterproof by using part of a plastic bottle as the label. If the pot is going to be inside, you can just use cardboard to make your label.

Riley's rosemary

Sarah's sage

Jesse's thyme

54

What to do:

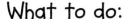

1. Once you've set up your craft station, **ask an adult** to cut the end off a plastic bottle for you.

2. Using the bottle as a guide, trace a circle onto your cardboard.

3. **Ask an adult** to cut out the cardboard circle and to stick the wooden skewer into the cardboard.

4. Glue the skewer and cardboard together.

5. While you are mixing your paint, think about what you want to paint on your label.

6. Carefully paint a pattern or picture onto your plant label.

7. When you are happy with your painting, add the plant name to the label and let your label dry.

8. It is important to keep your wet label somewhere high up away from animals and where no-one will touch it.

9. When your label is dry, stick it in the soil near your plant.

Make your own plant shapes

With just a little work, you can train vines to grow into amazing shapes. Have you ever wished that a rocket ship or even a rare and unusual animal would come to your garden? Well, now they can – just grow them!

What to do:

1. Using your picture as a reference, draw the basic outline of your shape on a big piece of paper.

2. **Ask an adult** to bend the wire into the shape you have drawn. They should be able to bend the wire over the piece of paper to get the shape just right.

3. When you are happy with the shape, **ask an adult** to plant the two ends of the wire deep into the soil near the two vine plants.

4. Twist the vines around the wire.

5. As the vines grow, train them by winding the new growth around the wire. Soon the wire will be completely covered by your plant!

6. When your plant gets too bushy, **ask an adult** to help you cut it back into shape.

You will need:

- A picture of the shape you want to create
- Some large pieces of paper
- A marker pen
- A plant pot filled with soil and two young vine plants
- Some topiary wire, or a metal coat hanger

Make your own scarecrow

Birds love fruit. So if you have fruit and you also have birds, you might want to make your very own scarecrow to keep birds away!

What to do:

1. **Ask an adult** to help you tie the two sticks into a cross shape using the pantyhose.

2. Dress your scarecrow on the wooden frame.

3. Fill the clothes with stuffing until plump.

4. Now tie the ends of the sleeves and pant legs so the stuffing won't fall out.

5. **Ask an adult** to hammer the wooden frame into the soil of the garden plot.

6. Using marker pens, draw the face of your scarecrow on one side of the pillowcase.

7. Fill the pillowcase with stuffing until it is round.

8. Now it's time to tie the head to the frame. You will need to **ask an adult** for help. Stick the pillowcase on top of the wooden frame. Make sure the top of the stick goes right into the pillowcase. Using string, tie the bottom of the pillowcase tightly to the stick.

9. Add your scarecrow's hat and you're finished!

You will need:

- Old clothes
- Gardening gloves
- Special composting worms called tiger worms, or red wrigglers
- Large polystyrene box with lid
- Four bricks
- Old newspapers
- Kitchen waste
- Garden waste, like lawn clippings, old plants, soil and manure
- Dry waste, like straw or shredded newspaper
- Watering can full of water

Make your own worm farm

Worm farms, like compost bins, create nutrient-rich compost for the garden. So you'll need only one or the other, not both. If you are trying to choose between a compost bin or a worm farm, ask yourself this question: would you like thousands of little pets? If the answer is yes, then get ready to build a worm farm!

What to do:

1 **Ask an adult** if you can set up your worm farm. Then find a nice shady spot in the garden for your wriggly friends.

2 **Ask an adult** to punch some holes in the bottom of the box and set the box on four bricks.

3 Soak the newspaper and lay it on the bottom of the box.

Your first full box should sit below the second box.

4 Add garden waste, then kitchen waste, and then your worms! Put the lid on the box.

5 Every time you add waste, cover it with a layer of moistened dry waste, like wet newspaper. It is important to keep the box moist – but not wet!

6 You will soon fill your box and the worms will help out too, by adding lots of new worms to the family. When the box is full, add another box on top and follow steps 1 to 5.

7 When you want compost, look in the bottom box. If there are worms and scraps on top, move them to the newer box. Then dig your trowel down to the bottom of the box. If the compost is dark and flaky, it's ready for the garden!

Don't put these things in your worm farm or compost bin:
- Meat
- Fish
- Bones
- Citrus, onion and garlic peels
- Dairy products
- Oil
- Glossy magazines
- Nappies
- Dog poo
- Cat litter

Thank-you, worms!

Make your own compost bin

Compost is a mixture of garden waste and food waste. Over time, the waste breaks down into a nutrient-rich meal for your soil and plants. Compost does for plants what vegetables do for you – it helps them grow up big and strong!

You will need:

- Old clothes
- Gardening gloves
- Kitchen waste
- Garden waste, like lawn clippings, old plants and soil
- Dry waste, like straw or shredded newspaper
- A big garbage bin with a lid
- Watering can full of water

What to do:

1. **Ask an adult** if you can set up a compost bin in the garden. Then collect all your materials and work outside in the area where the bin will stay.

2. **Ask an adult** to cut out the bottom of the bin and to make some air holes in the side of the bin.

3. Layer your waste in the bin: dry waste, then kitchen waste, and then garden waste. Now, water the pile of waste well and put on the bin lid.

4. Every time you have kitchen or garden waste, add it to the bin. Always cover the waste with a layer of dry waste and water well.

5. When your bin is full, mix the compost thoroughly. Now it's time to wait!

6. You will know your compost is ready for the garden when all the waste is completely broken down and the compost is dark and flaky.